A DAY IN THE LIFE
Big Cats

WHAT DO LIONS, TIGERS, AND PANTHERS GET UP TO ALL DAY?

Contents

Welcome to the world of big cats!

My name is Tyus D. Williams and I'm a wildlife scientist who studies **predators**, like some of the big cats in this book. I've loved big cats ever since I was a kid. Not only are they beautiful creatures with incredible skills, they also have an important role to play in the tough environments in which they live.

In this book I'm going to show you the daily activities of these incredible species, from lions on the plains of Africa to snow leopards trekking across the snowy mountaintops of Asia. Some of these cats start early in the morning, some nap during the day, and some are more active at night. By the end of the book you will have witnessed incredible hunting techniques, sweet moments between mothers and cubs, and spectacular fights.

Big cats are a fascinating group of animals. They demand respect from everyone, but in a changing world many are **threatened** by the prospect of losing their homes or being hunted. However, together we can unite to protect these species and their habitats and secure a future where we can live peacefully alongside these majestic creatures.

Tyus D. Williams

Lion

Tiger

Snow leopard

Leopard

Jaguar

Meet the family

All wild cats belong to the Felidae family and share a common ancestor. Over ten million years these cats split into different species, but they all share similar characteristics that you can still see today.

Cheetah

Puma

Puma branch

Cheetahs and pumas belong to a different branch of the cat family than the other big cats. The common ancestor of pumas and cheetahs lived 4.9 million years ago.

Panthera branch

This side of the cat family emerged 6.4 million years ago. It includes the five big cats shown above.

Family tree

Family trees are used to show how species split and changed from their common ancestor over millions of years. We don't know what the common ancestor of the big cats looked like!

Domestic cats

Have you ever wondered where your furry friend comes from? House cats descend from the same original ancestor as the big cats. They split from other cats in the family tree 3.4 million years ago. Like their giant cousins they are hunters (just ask the birds in your neighborhood).

Extinct cats

Saber-toothed tigers, also known as smilodons, were a prehistoric cat species that lived from 12 million years ago to 10,000 years ago. They roamed all over the world before going extinct, possibly at the hands of early human hunters. Saber-toothed tigers are distantly related to the Felidae family.

8AM The snow leopard freezes...

It's a brisk morning in the Himalayas, a gigantic mountain range in Central Asia. The air is still and silent. A snow leopard stalks along a ridge and comes across a **grazing markhor**, a large mountain goat. Her eyes light up—meals in the mountains are hard to come by. Hunching closer to the ground, using her silvery gray fur as **camouflage** to disguise herself against the snow, the snow leopard prepares for an attack.

With massive paws and dense fur, the snow leopard's feet act like **snowshoes**, muffling her steps. She inches closer and then makes her move, leaping toward the unsuspecting goat! Caution is needed though—hunting on steep mountains requires precision. One wrong step can result in a deadly 300-foot (90-meter) fall.

Snow leopards have
the longest jump in the
animal kingdom.

A tale of two cats

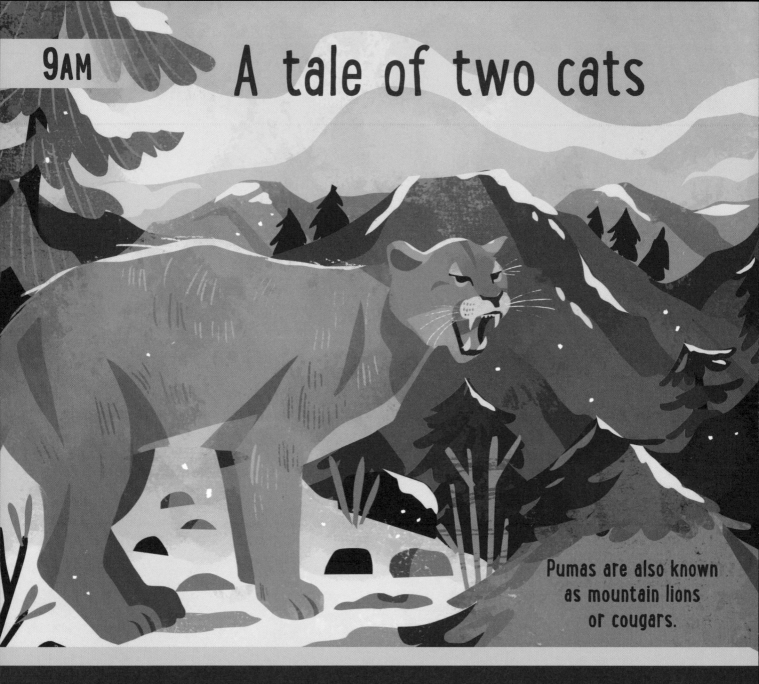

Pumas are also known as mountain lions or cougars.

High in the chilly peaks of Colorado, in the heart of the Rocky Mountains, a young male puma calls out into the vast landscape stretching before him. He wants any rival pumas to know that this is his territory—**be warned!**

The puma is the largest wild cat in the United States, and it's more closely related to cheetahs than lions or tigers. You'd be lucky to see a puma in the wild. But it's not just snowy mountains where they're found...

Down in the sweltering swamps of Florida, a female puma is on the move, creeping through sprawling tropical plants in search of something to eat—maybe a tasty raccoon.

Along the way she stops occasionally to **spray pee** against tree trunks and bushes. Scenting like this is a way of marking her territory—if you're unlucky you might have seen house cats do something similar! Pumas also yowl and screech to communicate with each other, because unlike most other big cats they can't roar.

The tiger picks up a scent

In the Great Plains of northern India, a large male tiger wanders through an open forest on the prowl. Youthful, strong, and curious, this tiger is in his prime. He has very little to fear from those who may dare to **challenge him**.

Stalking through the trees in absolute silence, he is practically invisible to any potential prey. His orange fur and black stripes blend in with tall grasses and leaves, making his outline hard to spot.

No two tigers have the same stripes.

Suddenly he stops at a tree that's giving off a **pungent smell**. Intrigued by the odor, he investigates by getting close and taking a big sniff. The scent is familiar but it has been a long time since he has interacted with the tiger who left it.

Responding, the tiger leaves his own mark by scratching near the base of the tree. Then he sprays pee to signal his presence, in case the mysterious individual passes by again.

Taking it easy after a long night

Slumbering high in the treetops of the Amazon rainforest in South America is a jaguar, but something is different about him. Rather than a golden coat with black spots, like most jaguars, this cat has a rare condition that causes his fur to be much darker. He's a **black panther!** And when hunting at night this can be a big advantage.

Last night, however, wasn't successful. And now the jaguar rests in the canopy. Wild cats nap frequently to conserve energy for important activities like hunting or traveling long

Meanwhile... In Africa, lions, elephants, and water buffalo gather together for a drink at a watering hole. It's not unusual to see lots of species gathering like this without fighting—especially when everyone's thirsty!

distances. Jaguars are **incredible climbers** and will often snooze high up where they can't be disturbed.

After our black panther rests for a few hours, he will be ready and alert to continue his journey, hopefully finding something to eat next time...

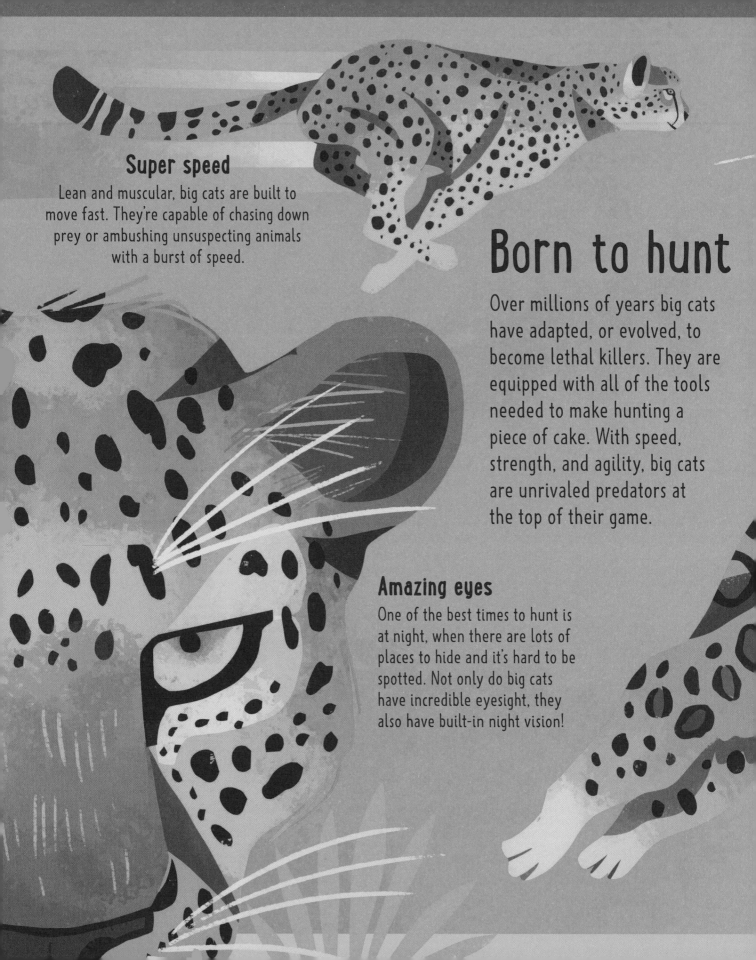

Super speed

Lean and muscular, big cats are built to move fast. They're capable of chasing down prey or ambushing unsuspecting animals with a burst of speed.

Born to hunt

Over millions of years big cats have adapted, or evolved, to become lethal killers. They are equipped with all of the tools needed to make hunting a piece of cake. With speed, strength, and agility, big cats are unrivaled predators at the top of their game.

Amazing eyes

One of the best times to hunt is at night, when there are lots of places to hide and it's hard to be spotted. Not only do big cats have incredible eyesight, they also have built-in night vision!

Powerful jaws

One of the most powerful tools big cats possess is their jaws. They're capable of exerting bone-crushing force on unfortunate prey.

Sensitive whiskers

Whiskers allow cats a super sense of touch as they navigate through their environment. They stretch out from the face and allow cats to feel just how wide spaces are as they squeeze through them.

Open wide! What's the point of having mighty jaws without long sharp teeth to bite with?

Sharp claws

Most big cats are equipped with razor-sharp claws that they can retract, or withdraw, when they're not using them. These claws allow them to climb trees and hold onto prey as they pounce on top of them.

Giant leap

With spring-loaded hind legs, snow leopards have the ability to leap more than 50 feet (15 meters) through the air and land as quietly as a mouse.

Clash of the snow leopards

Snow leopards can't roar. They yowl at each other instead.

Catching the markhor had been hard work, but now our snow leopard has a new challenge: how to keep it! In the frigid mountains of the Himalayas survival is everything, and sometimes that means competing against your own. A **rival snow leopard** approaches, and she's hungry too. The tension builds as they stare each other down. Fighting to protect this meal could be dangerous—the snow leopard has to be willing to risk injury for the reward of a full tummy.

As they circle each other the two cats screech with ear-piercing calls. Then, in a blur of movement, our snow leopard uses her spring-loaded hind legs to leap at the challenger. She worked hard for this meal and isn't giving it up easily. With a **menacing growl** and a couple of swipes with her large paws, she soon has her enemy running back the way she came. Our hero licks her wounds and goes back to her carcass. What a day this is turning out to be!

Hiding the catch

It's lunchtime in Kenya, a country in East Africa. A female leopard has had a successful morning's hunting, and now she'd like a bite to eat. Unlike most cats, the leopard chooses to take her lunch up into a tree. Here she will be **out of reach** of other hungry predators, such as hyenas, lions, and wild dogs.

In one quick movement the leopard hoists her meal—**a tasty gazelle**—up into the branches. Although she's significantly smaller than a lion, leopards are equipped with powerful jaws and a muscular build. She's more than capable of dragging large animals like the gazelle up the trunk of a tree.

Climbing backward, and with a **couple of grunts**, the leopard completes her task. Finally able to relax, she settles down to eat, out of the glaring sun.

Meanwhile... A gharial, a fish-eating member of the crocodile family, is sunbathing by a river. Suddenly it becomes aware of the tiger making his way along the bank. The gharial makes a quick dash into the river. Better to be safe than sorry!

The chase heats up

As the African savannah bakes under the blazing sun, a blur of color flashes by. A cheetah is in hot pursuit! This female has her sights set on a gazelle. There's a lot of pressure on her shoulders—she's not just hunting for herself. This mom is also responsible for **three hungry cubs**.

Strong and perfectly shaped for maximum speed, cheetahs are built to sprint for only a few seconds. Running so fast consumes a lot of energy, so they tire quickly. This means it's important to make every second count. As the cheetah sprints she uses her tail to **maintain balance**, twisting and turning to match the gazelle's rapid movements. Catching up to her prey, she tackles it from behind and the two animals collapse in a dusty heap. Luckily for this cheetah family today's hunt is a success.

Cheetahs are the fastest land animals on Earth, capable of speeds of up to 65 mph (105 kph)!

While mom is hunting, the cubs watch from afar, hiding from predators.

Making a splash

Danger is afoot as a shadowy figure prowls through the rainforest. The black panther is at the top of the food chain—afraid of nothing—and he's hungry. Arriving at a river, he stands on the bank and takes in the scene below.

Moving through the water is a **black caiman**, a member of the crocodile family. It swims by without noticing the dark beast above it. The jaguar crouches in anticipation. And then, at the perfect moment, he plunges into the water after the caiman! Both animals disappear from view, deep under the surface.

A couple of moments pass by
and then there's a huge splash.
The jaguar bursts out of the water
with the caiman in his mouth!

The caiman struggles, but its fate is sealed.
The jaguar's jaws are **too powerful** to
escape. He truly is the king of the jungle.

A world of cats

From swamps and deserts to mountains and tropical rainforests, big cats can be found all over the globe! Over millions of years of evolution they have adapted to succeed in all sorts of different environments.

Size them up

Not all big cats are the same size. The biggest are tigers and lions, while cheetahs and snow leopards have much smaller bodies.

Tiger

Lion

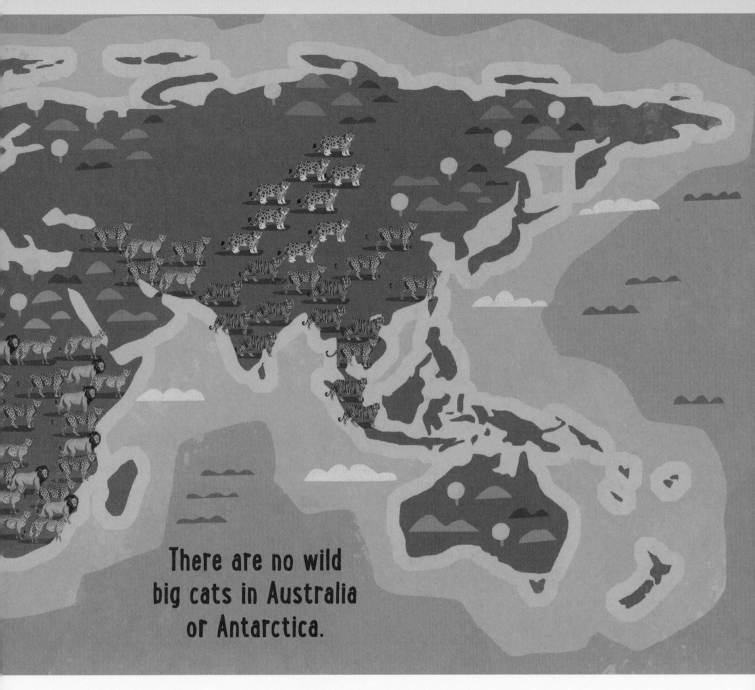

There are no wild
big cats in Australia
or Antarctica.

| Jaguar | Leopard | Puma | Cheetah | Snow leopard |

Dinner thieves

As the sun starts to set over the baking-hot grasslands of the African savannah, three lionesses pant after the hard work of taking down a **zebra**. However, their satisfaction is short-lived: A band of **spotted hyenas** has arrived in the mood for a free meal.

Hyenas look like dogs, but they're actually closely related to mongooses. Although lions are the largest meat-eaters, or **carnivores**, in Africa, these lionesses are clearly outnumbered. Hyenas form clans of up to 100 individuals, and they're not afraid of taking on lions.

Surrounded by howling hyenas, the lionesses have a decision to make. On another day it could be them stealing a meal from hyenas, but in this **perilous situation** they decide to make a quick retreat. A meal isn't worth dying over.

A touching reunion

A flock of birds bursts through the treetops as the tiger slowly swims across a marshy river. Reaching the far bank, he shakes off water droplets, and it isn't long before once again he picks up the scent. He tracks it for several more miles.

Eventually he finds the source of the smell—it's **his sister!** The two haven't seen each other since they were youngsters. Male tigers leave their moms earlier than females, ready to survive alone in the wild. Although it's been a while since he's seen his sister, he hasn't forgotten her scent. After a **brief touch of their noses** the siblings go their separate ways. Tigers from the same litter can have overlapping territories, but encounters like this are rare.

Meanwhile... Our black panther stumbles across a baby tapir. Fortunately for the youngster the panther is too full of caiman, and the tapir manages to escape back to the safety of its mother.

Cubs play fighting

With a growl, a cheetah cub launches herself at her brother. As they **tumble and roll** on the ground, their mom watches over them carefully. While it may look like harmless fun, play fighting can be the difference between survival and death for these cubs when they grow up. Learning how to pounce and grab each other helps them refine their hunting skills.

A short distance away in the long grass, a **mandrill** passes by. This is a potentially dangerous situation—cheetah cubs are vulnerable to animals like this monkey, especially when their mother is away hunting. Their best chance of survival is to stick with their mom until they are older and can take care of themselves. Sure enough, the presence of the adult cheetah stops the mandrill from attacking. The cubs are safe for now.

Lions, hyenas, and leopards are known to prey on cheetah cubs.

Meanwhile... Wandering through the Florida marshes, our puma stumbles across a large Burmese python. These gigantic snakes aren't from the United States originally—they're pets that escaped!

Wild dog siege

Africa has many predators, and if you think you can keep a good meal secret, you'd better think again. After filling her stomach, the leopard in the tree rests—but her peace is short-lived. **African wild dogs** notice her carcass, and they're hungry. Surrounding the tree, they begin to bark at the leopard in an attempt to scare her from her hard-won supper. The leopard is outnumbered, but she has one big advantage—wild dogs can't climb trees.

Eventually the leopard has had enough. She rushes down to a branch close to the ground and **roars** at the wild dogs. After a few exchanges back and forth, the wild dogs realize their chances of stealing a meal are small. They make a hasty retreat.

Meanwhile... The snow leopard patiently watches a group of bharal, also known as blue sheep, from the hills above them.

Staying hidden

The secret to being a master of hide-and-seek for these cats isn't just about technique, it's also about their fur! Each species has a special coat that allows them to blend into their surroundings. Swirls, spots, and stripes galore!

Lion

With a sandy brown coat and cream-colored underside, the fur of African lions mirrors the landscape of the African savannah.

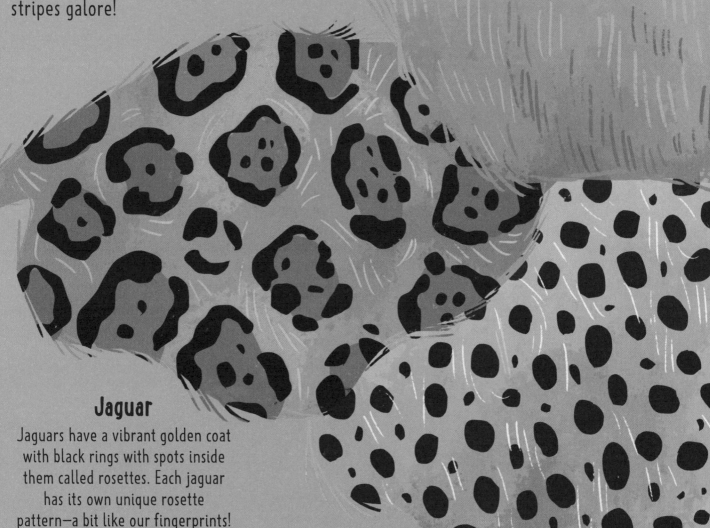

Jaguar

Jaguars have a vibrant golden coat with black rings with spots inside them called rosettes. Each jaguar has its own unique rosette pattern—a bit like our fingerprints!

Cheetah

Cheetahs are the only big cats that have spots without rosettes. As a cheetah sprints, its spots turn into a blur of black and gold.

Tiger

Tigers are the only big cat species with stripes. Perfect for hiding in long grass!

Snow leopard

With a pale gray coat, swirls of black rosettes, and a white underbelly, snow leopards blend in perfectly against the snow-covered mountains of Central Asia.

Leopard

Leopards have a similar coat to jaguars, but their rosettes lack central spots.

Puma

Pumas have light brown fur and a pale underside. However, their cubs have spots when they are born, which help them hide more effectively.

8PM The tiger approaches a farm

It's getting late and our tiger is hungry. As he steps out of the jungle he sees a farm full of cows, grazing without a care in the world. This presents a **dangerous situation** for the tiger, as well as for the locals who live in the nearby village. Like many predators, tigers are hunters who will take any opportunity that comes their way. Anything for a simple meal—and for the tiger, the cattle look like an easy target.

The farmers can't risk anything happening to their cows. They have to protect them in order to **feed their families**, even if that means risking their own lives or hurting the big cat. The tiger is spotted by the farmers and the village quickly gathers to drive the predator back into the forest by making lots of noise. There's no meal for the tiger, but he lives to see another day.

The best way to keep tigers safe is to protect their habitat so they're not forced to come into contact with humans.

Humans present a very real danger, so the tiger darts back into the jungle as quickly as possible.

The deer doesn't see the puma until it's too late.

Hunting in the night

Shhhhh! Don't move! Not even a muscle. When it comes to hunting, **stealth** and absolute silence are critical.

Luckily for the two pumas, they're perfectly adapted for hunting in their different environments. While one hides in a tree in the mountains, the other crouches in bushes in the swamps of Florida.

Pumas use a camouflage strategy called **countershading**. This means the color of their fur is different from top to bottom. On top they're a brown color, and they have a white underbelly. This is useful because when pumas are hiding in trees in the day, they're hard to see against the sunshine when viewed from below. At night, however, their brown fur perfectly blends into the shadows.

All of this added together is not good news for this elk or this deer...

Countershading is common in the animal world—it can also be seen in penguins and sharks.

An intruder approaches

There is always danger lurking across the plains of Africa, even for a pride of lions. As the lions sleep, the cubs huddle against their mothers for protection. Suddenly an intruder appears on the horizon, and he is not friendly.

A **lone male lion** is looking to claim a pride of his own. Sizing up the lions in front of him, he sees his chance. But first he has to defeat the male of the pride, who is quick to notice the unwelcome visitor.

A battle between the titans breaks out! Mighty roars echo through the warm savannah air. If this lone challenger manages to defeat his opponent, he'll be able to fight off the lionesses and **kill their cubs**—securing the pride for himself. Everything is about survival, and this lion is willing to do anything to gain power. Luckily the male of the pride is up to the fight, overpowering his challenger with his strength and aggression. The young male retreats. The pride is safe!

The lone male lion tries to sneak through the grass, but he is spotted.

A changing forest

In the dark of the night, the panther emerges from the bushes. As the years pass the jungle he calls home is **changing**. He walks into a clearing. Where once there were trees filled with insects, monkeys, and birds, now there are just ghosts of the past—logs and tree stumps everywhere, freshly cut by humans who want to sell the wood.

This process is called **deforestation**, and it's incredibly harmful. Clearing trees removes places for animals to find food and shelter. It will now take hundreds of years for this clearing to grow back. The Amazon is the largest tropical rainforest on the planet. It contains more than 30 percent of Earth's known species, and it's disappearing.

It's not too late for humans to save it, however. With better protection, animals like our panther will be free to continue living their amazing wild lives. A new generation of people protecting the planet is needed—will you join the fight to save the rainforest?

Glossary

Black panther
The name given to either a jaguar or a leopard who has a rare condition causing its fur to be black.

Camouflage
The ability of an animal or plant to blend into its environment to avoid being spotted.

Carcass
The dead body of an animal.

Carnivore
A meat-eater. All big cats are carnivores.

Coat
A name for the fur covering an animal.

Countershading
A camouflaging strategy used by some animals, where their top is a different color from their underside. This helps them to blend into their surroundings when seen from above or below.

Deforestation
The deliberate cutting down of forests by humans.

Ecosystem
The natural system in which animals and plants live and interact with one another and their environment.

Environment
The natural world, or the area where an animal or plant lives.

Evolution
How species change over time to better suit the environment they live in.

Extinct
Refers to a species of animal or plant that has died out and no longer exists on Earth.

Family tree
A diagram used to see how different species of animal are related to one another.

Felidae
The scientific name for the cat family.

Food chain
A simple way of describing the connections between different species that eat one another.

Habitat
The place where something lives.

Herbivore
A plant-eater.

Omnivore
An animal that eats meat and plants.

Predator
An animal that eats other animals (its prey).

Prey
An animal that is eaten by other animals (its predators).

Index

This has been a

NEON ◆ SQUID

production

I would like to dedicate this book to my mom and dad. You continuously made an effort to nurture my innate passion for wildlife—from buying me Zoobooks to calling me downstairs when The Jeff Corwin Experience *was on TV—even though it was an unfamiliar interest to you. Thanks for always patiently listening to me ramble on about wildlife and science. Your favorite scientist, Tyus.*

Author: Tyus D. Williams
Illustrator: Chaaya Prabhat
US Editor: Allison Singer

Neon Squid would like to thank:

Georgina Coles for proofreading.

Copyright © 2022 St. Martin's Press
120 Broadway, New York, NY 10271

Created for St. Martin's Press
by Neon Squid
The Stables, 4 Crinan Street,
London, N1 9XW

EU representative: Macmillan
Publishers Ireland Ltd,
1st Floor, The Liffey Trust Centre,
117-126 Sheriff Street Upper,
Dublin 1, D01 YC43

10 9 8 7 6 5 4 3 2 1

The right of Tyus D. Williams to be
identified as the author of this work
has been asserted in accordance
with the Copyright, Designs and
Patents Act, 1988.

Library of Congress Cataloging-in-
Publication Data is available.

Printed and bound by Vivar Printing
in Malaysia.

ISBN: 978-1-684-49207-7

Published in March 2022.

www.neonsquidbooks.com